**GUITAR ATLAS SERIES**

*Guitar Styles from Around the Globe*

# Japan

## Your passport to a new world of music

### BURGESS SPEED

Alfred, the leader in educational publishing, and the National Guitar Workshop, one of America's finest guitar schools, have joined forces to bring you the best, most progressive educational tools possible. We hope you will enjoy this book and encourage you to look for other fine products from Alfred and the National Guitar Workshop.

Alfred Publishing Co., Inc.
16320 Roscoe Blvd., Suite 100
P.O. Box 10003
Van Nuys, CA 91410-0003
**alfred.com**

ISBN-10: 0-7390-4303-X (Book & CD)
ISBN-13: 978-0-7390-4303-5 (Book & CD)

*This book was acquired, edited and produced
by Workshop Arts, Inc., the publishing arm of
the National Guitar Workshop.
Nathaniel Gunod, acquisitions, managing editor
Burgess Speed, senior editor
Matthew Liston, editor
Timothy Phelps, interior design
Barbara Smolover, interior illustrations
Ante Gelo, music typesetter
CD recorded by Collin Tilton at Bar None Studio, Northford, CT;
performed by Burgess Speed on a 1972 Martin D-28

Cynthia Sample, interior photographs (pages 18, 20, and 22)
Cover photographs: © istockphoto.com
Guitar courtesy of Martin Guitars*

# Contents

Track
1

A compact disc is included with this book. This disc can make learning with the book easier and more enjoyable. The symbol shown at the left appears next to every example that is on the CD. Use the CD to help ensure that you're capturing the feel of the examples, interpreting the rhythms correctly, and so on. The track number below the symbol corresponds directly to the example you want to hear. Track 1 will help you tune your guitar to this CD.

# About the Author

**Burgess Speed** is the senior editor for National Guitar Workshop Publications. He is also an award-winning author (ARSC 2005 Best Research in Recorded Classical Music; *Leroy Anderson: A Bio-Bibliography*), musician, performer, and educator. He graduated *summa cum laude* from Western Connecticut State University with a B. A. in music (concentration in classical guitar). A trip to Thailand in 2001 sparked a keen interest in Asian culture and music, which led to the writing of this book. Burgess lives in Connecticut with his wife Kimberly and their four children.

## ACKNOWLEDGEMENTS

My deepest gratitude and admiration go to my beautiful wife Kimberly, for all of her love and support; also to Jack, Spencer, Holden, and Delaney, for their inspiration, love, excitement, and beautiful noise. Thanks also to Mom, Dad, Gram and Gram, Linda and Mark; and to Eleanor Anderson, Nat Gunod, Dave and Barbara Smolover, Ian Forbes, Gayle Pemberton, Tor Somlo, Mariko Matsumura, Bill Sample, Timothy Phelps, Matthew Liston, Donny Trieu, Link Harnsberger, Ron Manus, Kevin O'Neil, Collin Tilton, Steve Sauvé, Vladimir Aleandro, and the great professor of Asian studies Jack Sikora.

# Notation Key

H = Hammer-on.

P = Pull-off.

SL = Ascending slide.

SL = Descending slide.

¼ = Quarter-step bend.

⌢ = *Fermata.* Pause, or hold note longer than its indicated duration.

> = *Accent.* Emphasize the note or chord.

= *Arpeggiate.* Quickly roll the chord with the right-hand fingers or thumb.

↑ = Accented downstroke.

↓ = Accented upstroke.

Roman numerals: I = one; II = two; III = three; IV = four; V = five; VI = six; VII = seven; VIII = eight; IX = nine; X = ten.

BV₃ = In this example, barre three strings at the 5th fret.

BV = Barre all six strings at the 5th fret.

HBV = *Hinge barre* at the 5th fret. Play an individual note on the 1st string with the bottom of the 1st finger, just above the palm. Usually simplifies the next fingering.

*p, i, m, a* = The right-hand fingers starting with the thumb.

1, 2, 3, 4, 0 = The left-hand fingers starting with the index finger; 0 = open string. The left-hand fingers are indicated under the TAB.

*D.C. al Fine* = *Da Capo al Fine.* Go back to the beginning of the piece and play to the *Fine*, which is the end of the piece.

*Harm.* = *Harmonic.* Notes of the harmonic series that are very pure and clear. In this book, written at the sounding pitch with a diamond shaped notehead. Touch the string lightly over the indicated fret and pluck, immediately removing the finger from the string.

*molto* = Very much.

*poco a poco* = Little by little.

*rit.* = Abbreviation for *ritardando.* Become gradually slower.

*accelerando* = Become gradually faster.

*a tempo* = Return to the original tempo.

**Capo V** = Place the capo at the 5th fret. Standard music notation and TAB are written as if in open position. In other words, for easier reading, *true* pitch is not indicated.

*Swing 8ths* = Eighth notes written like straight eighth notes, but played like triplets with the first two eighth notes tied (♫ = ♫³). Swing eighth notes produce a shuffle feel.

①②③④⑤⑥ = The guitar strings, starting from the highest-pitched string, the 1st string, high E.

♩ = **88** = Tempo marking. In this case, there are 88 quarter notes, or beats, per minute. (If you have a metronome, set it to 88).

♪ = *Tremolo.* Rapidly strum the chord, alternating between downstrokes and upstrokes for the indicated duration.

# Introduction

Welcome to *Guitar Atlas: Japan.* Japan is known as the "Land of the Rising Sun." Situated in the Pacific Ocean to the east of Korea, China, and Russia, it consists of four main islands and over 3000 smaller islands. From north to south, the main islands are: Hokkaido, Honshu (the largest island, known as the Japanese *mainland*), Shikoku, and Kyushu. Japan is divided into 47 jurisdictions, or *prefectures.* The Tokyo Prefecture (which includes Tokyo, the nation's capitol) is located on the eastern coast of Honshu and is considered one of the largest metropolitan areas in the world.

Traditional Japanese music, or *hogaku,* is rich in many ways. It is complex, often highly structured, and has a philosophical and artistic depth that could take a lifetime to grasp. It can also be simple, earthy, inspirational, and enjoyable to Western musicians and non-musicians alike. This book is a modest introduction to the many faces of hogaku. A Brief History of Japanese Music is followed by a look at Traditional Instruments of Japan. Following this is a look at traditional Japanese Scales and Modes, including the interesting philosophy behind the pentatonic scale. Japanese Folk Music is covered, which is followed by the Classical Music of Okinawa, Shamisen Music of the Kabuki Theater, and then Koto Music.

The music in this book was not originally played on the guitar, but on the shamisen, sanshin, koto, shakuhachi, and other traditional Japanese instruments. Adapting this music to the guitar presents a significant challenge: there are the various tunings of the shamisen and koto (which were often altered in the middle of a piece), the fretless fingerboards of the shamisen and biwa, the absence of traditional harmony, etc. With the exception of one piece ("Kiso Bushi," page 22), the arrangements in this book are all fingerstyle. Various techniques have been used, like the *cross-string* style (see page 18), to emulate the sound of the koto, as well as new tunings derived from traditional Japanese tunings (see page 47). A capo is also employed in several examples to bring the pitch of the guitar closer to the shamisen and koto while retaining a "cross-string" feel. (These pieces can also be played without a capo). However, it should be remembered that the musical examples in this book are *arrangements.* Certain liberties have been taken with rhythm, notes, harmony, etc., to keep the music interesting, enjoyable, and repertoire friendly. However, the goal throughout has been to maintain the original integrity of the music, never sacrificing essence for accessibility.

This book is intended for intermediate to advanced guitarists who can read standard music notation and tablature (TAB) and who know a fair amount of technique and theory. Even if you can't read standard music notation, you can still get a lot out of this book. You can read the TAB and listen to the CD to help you figure out the music. Use the Notation Key on page 3 to help you with some potentially unfamiliar symbols. Also, if you just want to kick back and read, you will get interesting glances at the forces and personalities behind the music. So, take your time and enjoy.

# Chapter 1     BRIEF HISTORY OF JAPANESE MUSIC

JAPAN

Let's start by looking at the history of Japanese music in the context of Japan's historical periods.

## Early Ancient Period (6th Century and Prior)

In the *Early Ancient* period, Japan's music consisted only of songs.
Little is known of this ancient music. Society at this time consisted of a primitive system of clans and slave labor.

## Later Ancient Period (7th–10th Centuries)

The *Later Ancient* period, which encompassed the *Asuka, Nara,* and *Early Heian* periods, was a time when Japan was infused with the culture and music of other countries, especially China, Korea, and India. During this time, the clan system became more organized and governments were formed. The primary music of this period was known as *gagaku* ("elegant music"). Gagaku is a highly sophisticated music that was played only in the Imperial Courts. Another type of music that came into existence during this period is *shomyo,* the musical chanting of prayers and scripture by Buddhist priests.

## Early Middle Ages (11th–16th Centuries)

In the *Early Middle Ages* (which encompassed the *Later Heian, Kamakura,* and *Muromachi* periods), two new and important musical genres came into prominence: *heikebiwa* and *Noh.* Heikebiwa was a type of *narrative* music that consisted of long tales accompanied by the biwa. (For more on heikebiwa and the biwa itself, see page 8.) Noh was a new type of theater that fused the best elements of theater, dance, music, and literature. Society and the arts during this period were supported and controlled by *samurai* (feudal warriors) and Buddhist priests. The government itself was known as a *shogunate* (feudal government).

## Later Middle Ages (17th Century–1867)

The *Later Middle Ages* encompassed the *Momoyama* and *Edo* periods. (Edo was the ancient name of Tokyo.) The major musical genres of this era were associated with artisans, merchants, and peasants (considered the "lower classes" of feudal society relative to the samurai and Buddhist priests). The new genres were *shamisen music, koto music,* and *shakuhachi music.* These instruments and the genres they inspired are covered in the next chapter and throughout the book. In the later Edo period, these three types of music flourished and became extremely popular. It was also during this time that *Kabuki* theater and its music came into full flower. The *Ryukyu Kingdom,* which included the island of Okinawa, came under Japanese control in the 17th century; with this came a rich cultural heritage all its own. Another point worth mentioning is that, although folk music existed prior to this time, most known folk songs can be traced back to the beginning of the Edo period or more modern times.

## Modern Period (1867–Present)

The *Modern* period began with the Meiji Revolution in 1867. With the institution of the Meiji Government, the doors of Japan were opened to the West. Traditional music declined for a period in favor of European instruments, theory, and composition. But since World War II, Japan has experienced a resurgence of interest and appreciation for its native music and culture.

# Chapter 2   TRADITIONAL INSTRUMENTS OF JAPAN

**JAPAN**

## SHAMISEN AND SANSHIN

Perhaps the most popular of all traditional Japanese instruments is the *shamisen* (see illustration to the right), a banjo-like instrument with three strings. The shamisen is a relative of the Chinese *san-hsien* (literally, "three strings"), which first appeared in the Ryukyu Islands in the 14th century and found its way to mainland Japan around 1562. The instrument exists in present-day Okinawa as the *sanshin* (see illustration at bottom right), which, along with the Chinese *san-hsein* are covered with snakeskin. In mainland Japan, however, where snakeskin was not as plentiful, cat and dog skin were used.

The strings of the shamisen are sounded with a *bachi,* or plectrum, shaped like a ginkgo tree leaf. There are different sizes of shamisens, as well as plectrums, that produce a broad spectrum of tonal possibilities. A distinctive sound is produced when proper shamisen technique is used; the plectrum strikes the skin covering the body of the instrument almost simultaneously with the string, creating a kind of percussive effect. In Okinawa, the sanshin is played with a fingerpick on the index finger.

*Bachi.*

### Tunings

There are three primary tunings for the shamisen: *honchoshi, niagari,* and *sansagari.*

Honchoshi is the "standard," basic tuning and mood.

**Honchoshi**

*Shamisen.*

Niagari means "2nd string raised" a whole step. This tuning presents a brighter mood.

**Niagari**

Sansagari means "3rd string lowered" a whole step and produces a sadder, more introspective mood. (The 3rd string on the shamisen is the highest-pitched string.)

**Sansagari**

*Fingerpick.*

In traditional Japanese music, tunings are often changed in the middle of a piece to alter the mood.

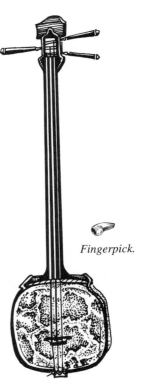

*Sanshin.*

## KOTO

The *koto* is a 13-string "floor harp" made of pawlonia wood, with strings traditionally made of silk. It is about six feet long and is traditionally played while sitting on the floor. The strings are plucked with ivory fingerpicks placed on the thumb, index, and middle fingers. The predecessor of the koto was the Chinese *guzheng,* which was introduced to Japan in the eighth century. At this time, the *so* (as the koto was known) became an integral part of the gagaku ensemble. The koto was rarely used for solo performance until the 17th century, when Yatsuhashi Kengyo began to compose solo music for the koto and popularized it as a solo instrument (for more on Yatsuhashi Kengyo, see page 40).

*Koto player.*

### Tunings

Following are the most common koto tunings (*hirajoshi, kumoijoshi,* and *kokinjoshi*), which are based on the *In* and *Yo* modes (see Chapter 3, page 10).

### Hirajoshi

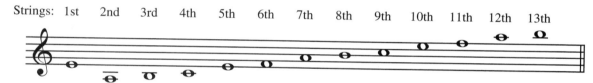

### Kumoijoshi

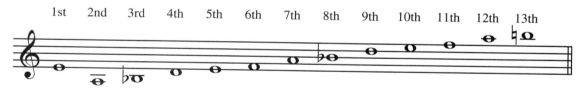

### Kokinjoshi

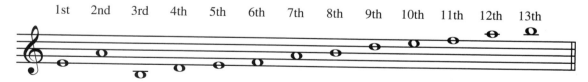

## BIWA

The *biwa* is a four-string lute with a flat back and silk strings. Like the shamisen, sanshin, and koto, the biwa came to Japan by way of China. The instrument was originally used by blind Buddhist priests to accompany their prayers and chanting. The strings, which are very high off the fingerboard, are plucked with a large plectrum, or *bachi*. The notes are sounded by pressing a left-hand finger directly on top of one of the frets. Because there are not many frets, notes are also produced by pressing in *between* the frets. As you can see in the illustration to the right, the frets are high off the fingerboard; because of this, the string does not make contact with the neck, so the pitch of the note is determined by how hard the finger is pressed.

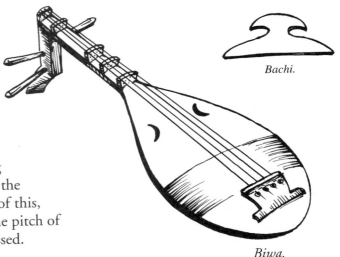

*Bachi.*

*Biwa.*

In addition to being used as accompaniment by Buddhist priests, the biwa also inspired a type of narrative music called *heikebiwa*. This important genre consisted of epic songs about the rise and fall of the powerful Heike clan, which disappeared in A.D. 1185. Although shamisen music largely overshadowed and eventually replaced biwa music, the instrument itself has remained an essential part of traditional Japanese music.

## SHAKUHACHI

The *shakuhachi* is an end-blown flute made of bamboo. The instrument has strong connections to Buddhism, having made its way from China to Japan in A.D. 590, at which time it was played by wandering Buddhist priests in search of alms. The shakuhachi is used to inspire and enhance contemplation and meditation. Ironically, in more warlike times, it was used by some Buddhist priests as a weapon. The shakuhachi has five holes, which, through various fingerings and blowing techniques, can produce all the tones in the Japanese musical system (for more on these tones, see Traditional Scales and Modes, page 10). By adjusting the blowing angle while playing a note, pitch bends and slides can be produced. Though the shakuhachi is an integral part of many genres of traditional Japanese music, there is a genre known as *honkyoku* that consists solely of solo shakuhachi music. Honkyoku is characterized by *free rhythm* (no time signature) and melodies based on the *In* mode (see page 13).

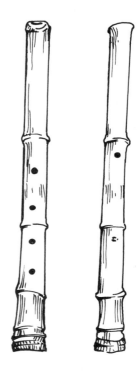

*Shakuhachi
(top and bottom).*

## TAIKO, GAKUDAIKO, AND DADAIKO

The *taiko* is a big drum with animal hide stretched and nailed across its top and bottom. It sits on a stand, and varies in size according to the type of music being played. A smaller, or shallower, taiko is called a *gakudaiko.* There is also a very large version—the *dadaiko*—known for its volume and beautiful tone. Taiko drums, which are popular in Japan even today, are said to have been used on battlefields to strike fear into the enemy with their thunderous sounds.

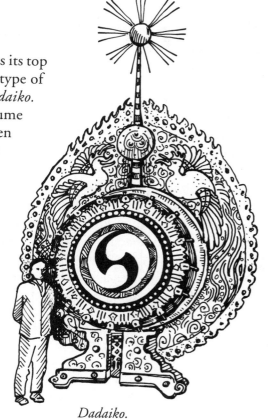

*Taiko player.*

*Gakudaiko.*

*Dadaiko.*

## TSUZUMI

The *tsuzumi* is a two-headed drum in the shape of an hourglass. The heads (originally made of fox skin) are laced together with the body of the drum in between. Tsuzumi drums are played by holding the drum to the right shoulder with the left hand, and tapping the head with the right-hand fingers. The volume and pitch of the drum is controlled by pulling on the tension cords. The tsuzumi is known also as *kotsuzumi* ("small tsuzumi") when it is played with the larger version known as the *otsuzumi.*

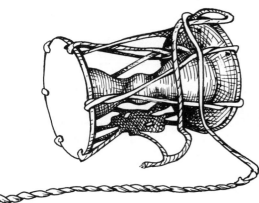

*Tsuzumi.*

## BINZASARA

*Binzasara* are wooden clappers. They consist of pieces of wood held together by string. These pieces of wood clap against each other when the player, holding the handles about a shoulder's width apart, brings his/her hands toward each other. Binzasara are used in folk music and music of the Kabuki theater.

*Binzasara player.*

# Chapter 3 TRADITIONAL SCALES AND MODES

JAPAN

In this chapter, we'll be looking at the most commonly used scales, or *modes* (as they are often called), in koto, shamisen, shakuhachi, and traditional folk music. Like Western scales, traditional Japanese scales and modes are based on a system of 12 tones (though the actual pitches differ slightly from their Western counterparts).

There are two types of Japanese scales: 1) the "hard," or *Yo,* modes, and 2) the "soft," or *In,* modes. The terms *Yo* and *In* correspond to the Chinese *Yang* (masculine principle) and *Yin* (feminine principle). Further, a masculine or feminine quality is ascribed to every note in a scale.

The *Yo* and *In* modes are *pentatonic,* or "five-tone," scales, and they are the basis for most traditional Japanese music (with the exception of the seven-tone *ryo* and *ritsu* scales and modes used in gagaku).

## SCALE AND MODE THEORY

Japanese music theory was heavily influenced by ancient Chinese music theory, which held that each tone of the pentatonic scale was related to one of the five elements: *Wood–Fire–Earth–Metal–Water.* The chart below shows the relationships between these elements and the notes of the scale, which are named: *kyu–sho–kaku–chi–u.* The order of the scale tones is intimately connected to the procession of elements as they either engender or conquer one another according to the Chinese philosophy of "change."

| | The Cornerstone | | | | |
|---|---|---|---|---|---|
| Elements | Wood | Fire | Earth | Metal | Water |
| Japanese scale tones | kaku | chi | kyu | sho | u |
| Position in scale | 3rd | 4th | 1st | 2nd | 5th |

In the chart above, notice that the 3rd note of the scale is referred to as the *cornerstone.* This is the most important note because wood is symbolic of spring, new beginnings, and the supreme virtue of benevolence. Unlike Western music theory, which is based on the *tonic,* or first note, Japanese theory is based on the 3rd, or middle, note of the scale. The cornerstone acts as the musical "home base," or "tonal center," and its position in the scale reflects this function.

Now, let's look at some actual scales. We will use the Japanese designations for scale tones. The reason we will not use Western scale degrees (1–♭3–4–5–♭7, etc.) is because they will not accurately represent the nature of the scale. Remember, in the Western system, the 1st note, or tonic, is the most important note. But, in the Japanese system, the 3rd note, or cornerstone, is the most important. In the Japanese system, when the pitch of a note is raised, it is given the prefix "ei." For example, when the 2nd tone, *sho,* is raised, it becomes *ei-sho.* The *intervals,* or distances, between the scale tones will be indicated in the following way:

    H   = *Half step* (one fret)

    W   = *Whole step* (two frets)

 W+H  = *Whole step plus half step* (three frets)

  2W   = *Two whole steps* (four frets)

## THE *YO* MODES

We will look at three forms of the *Yo* mode. What is characteristic of these modes is there are no half steps. The *Yo* modes were often used for "simple" folk songs. The most basic form—we'll call it *Form 1*—consists of: *kyu–sho–kaku–chi–u–(kyu)*. (For a sense of finality, the first note of the scale will be repeated at the end.)

### *Yo* Mode—Form 1

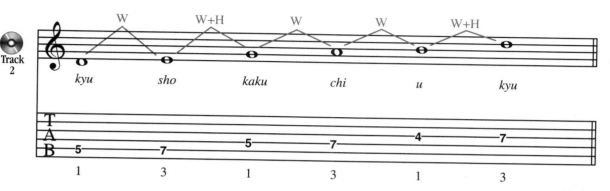

In *Form 2* of the *Yo* mode, the 5th tone, *u*, is raised and becomes *ei-u*.

### *Yo* Mode—Form 2

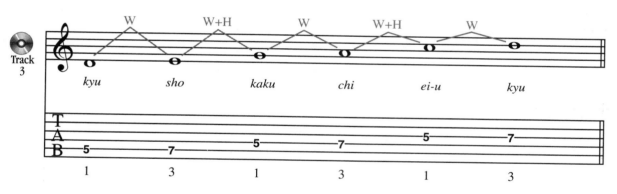

In *Form 3* of the *Yo* mode, *ei-sho* takes the place of *sho*, and *ei-u* takes the place of *u*.

### *Yo* Mode—Form 3

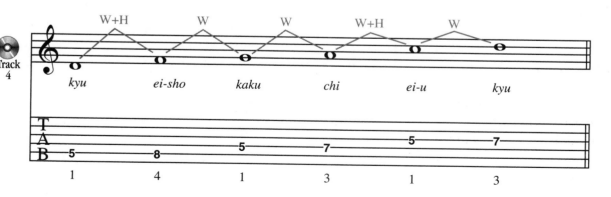

You may notice that the above mode bears a close resemblance to the classic D Minor Pentatonic scale.

It is common in traditional Japanese music to use Form 2 ascending and Form 1 descending. This resembles how the melodic minor scale is used in Western Baroque and Classical music.*

### Yo Mode

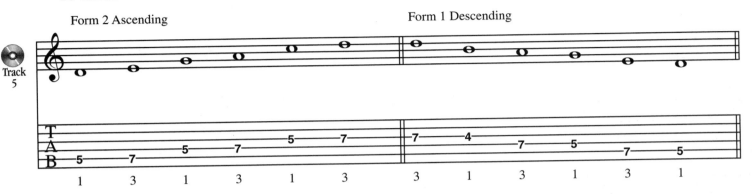

The melodic system above was used in composing the Japanese national anthem, "Kimi Ga Yo" (see page 21 for a full arrangement).

**Excerpt from "Kimi Ga Yo"**

Following is a two-octave version for you to experiment with on your guitar. Notice the use of slides for shifting to new positions. Also, notice the *grace note* in measure 4. A grace note (♪) is a tiny, ornamental note that precedes the main note. As soon as a grace note is played, you quickly go to the main note (in this case, *pull off* to the main note).

### Yo Mode—Two Octaves

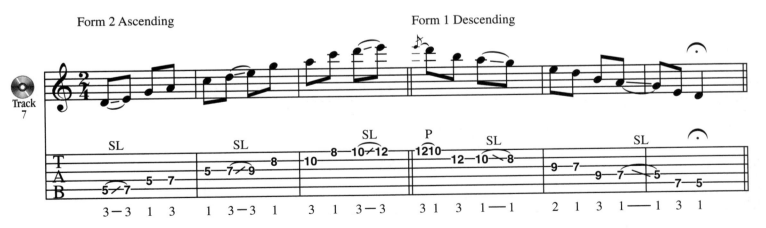

* The melodic minor scale is played 1–2–♭3–4–5–6–7 ascending, and ♭7–♭6–5–4–♭3–2–1 descending.

## THE *IN* MODES

The defining characteristic of the *In* modes is the presence of half steps. These modes were often used for more sophisticated music, including the music of the koto and shamisen, and folk music based on these. We will look at three forms of the *In* mode. The basic form—*Form 1*—consists of: *kyu–sho–kaku–chi–u–(kyu)*. Notice the names for the scale tones in the *Yo* and *In* modes are the same.

### *In* Mode—Form 1

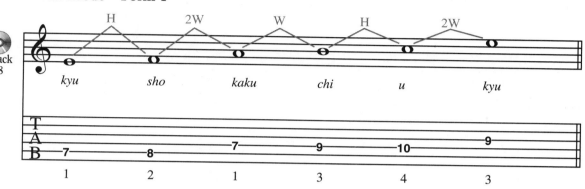

This is the mode used in the famous Japanese song "Sakura" (see page 18 for a full arrangement). Notice that the note A, which is the 3rd tone in the scale, is the tonal center of this melody.

**Excerpt from "Sakura"**

In *Form 2* of the *In* mode, *u* is raised to become *ei-u*.

### *In* Mode—Form 2

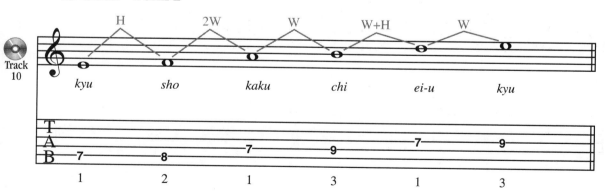

In *Form 3* of the *In* mode, *ei-sho* takes the place of *sho*, and *ei-u* takes the place of *u*. (Although there are no half steps in Form 3, it is still considered an *In* mode because it is derived from the *In* mode's basic form (Form 1).

### *In* Mode—Form 3

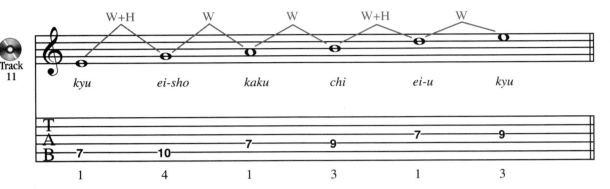

Notice that the above scale closely resembles an E Minor Pentatonic scale.

Similar to the *Yo* mode, Form 2 is often used when ascending, and Form 1 is used descending.

### *In* Mode

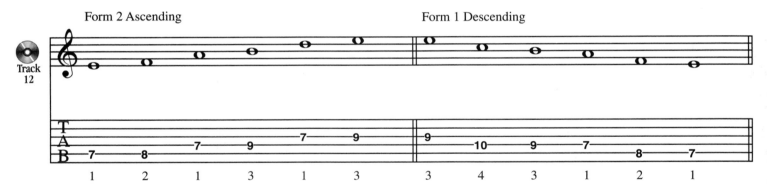

Following is a two-octave version to play on your guitar.

### *In* Mode—Two Octaves

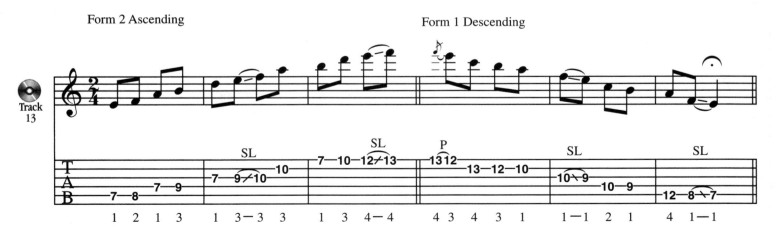

14

## THE HIRAJOSHI, KUMOIJOSHI, AND KOKINJOSHI "SCALES"

The *hirajoshi*, *kumoijoshi*, and *kokinjoshi* "scales" are Western derivations of the koto tunings of the same names (see page 7). These scales have been used by rock and jazz guitarists in search of "new" sounds.

The *hirajoshi* "scale" (A–B–C–E–F–A) is like Form 1 of the *In* mode (E–F–A–B–C–E), just starting from a different note (A instead of E).

**Hirajoshi "Scale"**

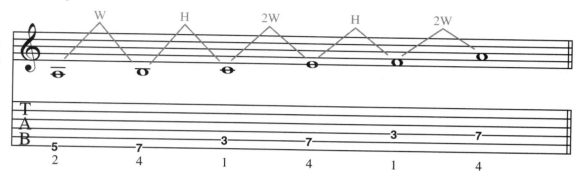

The *kumoijoshi* "scale" (A–B♭–D–E–F–A) is also like Form 1 of the *In* mode. Remember, the step pattern for Form 1 (as well as this kumoijoshi "scale") is: H–2W–W–H–2W. So, it is like Form 1 of the *In* mode in another "key," or with another tonal center.

**Kumoijoshi "Scale"**

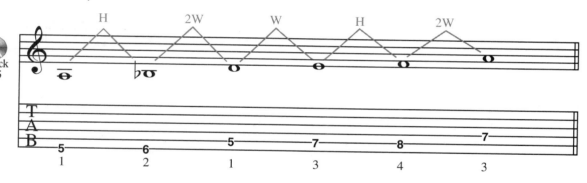

The *kokinjoshi* "scale" (B–D–E–F–A–B) is like Form 2 of the *In* mode (E–F–A–B–D–E), but starting on B.

**Kokinjoshi "Scale"**

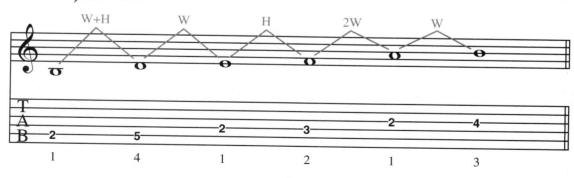

There is a lot in this chapter to work with and study. Feel free to experiment with different fingerings and applications in your own music. In the next chapter, we'll look at some traditional folk music and start playing some arrangements.

# Chapter 4　　FOLK MUSIC (MINYO)

The term *minyo* encompasses all Japanese folk music. There are many other designations for this genre, including *hina uta, inaka bushi,* and *inaka buri,* all of which can be roughly translated as "country songs." However, throughout history, and to most performers of the music, traditional folk tunes are simply referred to as *uta* (songs). Japanese folk music can be divided into the following categories:

- **Religious songs.** These include *sato kagura,* songs usually sung at country shrines accompanied by the *shinobue* (a high-pitched, side-blown flute) and taiko drums of various sizes. *Bon-uta,* or music used for Bon dances (see page 22), also fall into this category.

- **Work songs.** These include songs for rice planting, sake making, fishing, etc. Many of these songs were unaccompanied and were sung solo or in groups. It was common for them to feature a kind of *call and response* similar to early African-American songs.

- **Songs for celebrations and gatherings.** Included in this category are songs for parties and feasts.

- **Songs for weddings and funerals.**

- **Lullabies and children's songs.** These include traditional songs passed on from generation to generation *(warabe uta)* as well as songs written in the 20th century *(doyo).*

## MELODIES

Folk melodies are usually sung in the *In* and *Yo* modes. As mentioned on page 11, the simpler melodies are in the *Yo* mode, while the melodies in the *In* mode tend to be a bit more sophisticated and even influenced by classic shamisen music. Many of the simpler melodies do not span more than an octave.

## SINGING

The singing in Japanese folk music is dynamic and often quite highly charged. There are vocal slides from note to note, with long melodic passages on a single syllable (in Western music, this is known as *melisma*). There are other effects used such as *kakegoe,* or pitched calls and shouts.

## RHYTHM

There are two types of rhythm used in minyo: *free* and *metered.* Metered rhythm is found in work songs, songs used for dances, and children's songs. There is a type of song known as *ondo* that has a distinct rhythm. It has a $\frac{2}{4}$ "swing" feel to it. Many songs used for Bon dances fall into this category, as is the case with "Kiso Bushi" (page 22). Free rhythm is found in unaccompanied songs for work and entertainment, or songs accompanied by the shakuhachi rather than drums and shamisen.

## THE INSTRUMENTS

Instruments used to play minyo vary greatly. Taiko drums and drums of all types and sizes are used, as well as a gong called a *kane,* and different kinds of bells and binzasara. Also used are the shamisen (and in Okinawa, the sanshin), koto, and shakuhachi. A full instrumental folk ensemble is known as *hayashi.* The term "hayashi" is derived from the word that means to "play and make happy." The musical ensembles in both Noh and Kabuki are also known as *hayashi.*

## FOLK MUSIC TODAY

Folk songs vary from region to region, with each area having its own styles and beloved melodies. Today, even though mass media has rendered *all* folk music accessible to everyone in Japan, the music from one's hometown or region will still touch a person deeply and make them nostalgic for home and family.

## "EDO KOMORI-UTA"

*Komori-uta* is Japanese for "lullaby." This simple, yet beautiful cradle song from the Edo period is about a baby whose nursemaid has gone home over the mountains to her own village. In some versions, she is to return with a flute and drum for the child; in other versions, it's unclear whether or not she will return.

The arrangement below features *double stops* in the melody (double stops are two notes played at the same time). Most of these are plucked with the *i* and *m* fingers of the right hand. Pay attention to the double-stop slide in measure 6; the two starting notes are grace notes. So, as soon as you play the first double stop, you quickly slide to the main notes.

**EDO KOMORI-UTA**
(Edo Lullaby)

Track 17

## "SAKURA"

"Sakura" is a famous and beloved Japanese folk song. Its melody was written in the Edo period for young students of the koto; the words as they now appear were added in the Meiji period. The word *sakura* means "cherry blossoms." Sakura is the national flower of Japan; it is also the name for the season of spring.

### Cross-String Technique

The following arrangement uses the *cross-string* technique, where melodic and harmonic lines are *phrased,* or fingered, in such a way as to keep notes ringing. Instead of playing a succession of notes on a single string, you go back and forth to create a *harp-like effect.* This effect is reminiscent of the sound of the koto. Measures 1, 3, and 4 are great examples of this. Also, make sure you hit the harmonics in measures 2 and 22.

*Sakura, or "cherry blossoms," the national flower of Japan.*

## "KIMI GA YO"

"Kimi Ga Yo" is the national anthem of Japan. Though it has been the unofficial anthem since the Meiji period, it became the official anthem in 1999 with the passing of the Law Concerning the National Flag and Anthem.

### The Words

The title can be translated as "Imperial Reign" or "Emperor's Reign." The words are from an anonymous poem written in the Heian period. Roughly, they can be translated as:

*May your Imperial Reign last forever,*
*Until the pebbles become boulders,*
*covered by moss.*

In the Heian period, it was believed that with the passage of time, pebbles could become boulders.

### The Music

This poem was used in songs of celebration by people throughout Japan before being chosen as the lyrics for the national anthem in 1869. After a failed first attempt at a melody composed by a visiting Irish band leader (Western music and culture were held in high regard during the Meiji period), a new melody was composed in 1880 under the supervision of Hiromori Hayashi. This melody was harmonized in a Western style by Franz von Eckert, a German musician, and this is the version that has been in use ever since.

### The Controversy

Controversy has long surrounded "Kimi Ga Yo." For many Japanese, it is a symbol (along with the national flag) of Japan's imperialistic and militaristic past. School teachers and principals have even rebelled against a mandate to sing the anthem in schools. However, this noble-sounding anthem has its own important place in the history and music of Japan.

The arrangement on page 21 is in the style of Franz von Eckert's work from 1880. Watch the bass line in measure 5; it leads to chord voicings high up on the fretboard. If you don't have a cutaway model guitar, this can be a bit tricky.

Hinomaru, *Japan's national flag. The term Hinomaru means "sun disc." The large red disc is said to represent the rising sun.*

## KIMI GA YO
### (Japan's National Anthem)

## "KISO BUSHI"

Every summer, the festival of *Bon* is celebrated throughout Japan. Bon is a Buddhist holiday honoring the souls of departed ancestors. During the festival, there are *Bon odori* (Bon dances). These are events in which the people gather—in many cases traveling back to their hometowns from the larger cities—to celebrate with special songs *(Bon-uta)* and dances. These songs and dances are unique to each region. Many lanterns are lit during the Bon dances; originally, this was to lead the spirits home from the land of the dead, and then back again when the festivities were over.

The term *bushi* means "song" or "tune" with a distinctive melody. "Kiso Bushi" is an old folk song—with its own accompanying Bon dance—from the Kiso Mountain district. Kiso Mountains, otherwise known as the Central Alps, are a wooded mountain range in the heart of the Japanese mainland.

The melody of this song, which is quite distinctive, is in the *Yo* mode (see page 11). The guitar is tuned to *niagari* tuning (see page 47). Bends, hammer-ons, and pull-offs are used to emulate a singer's voice. This piece can be played fingerstyle, but to really bring out the quality of the shamisen's tone, try using a thin pick.

*Lanterns hung during the Buddhist festival of Bon.*

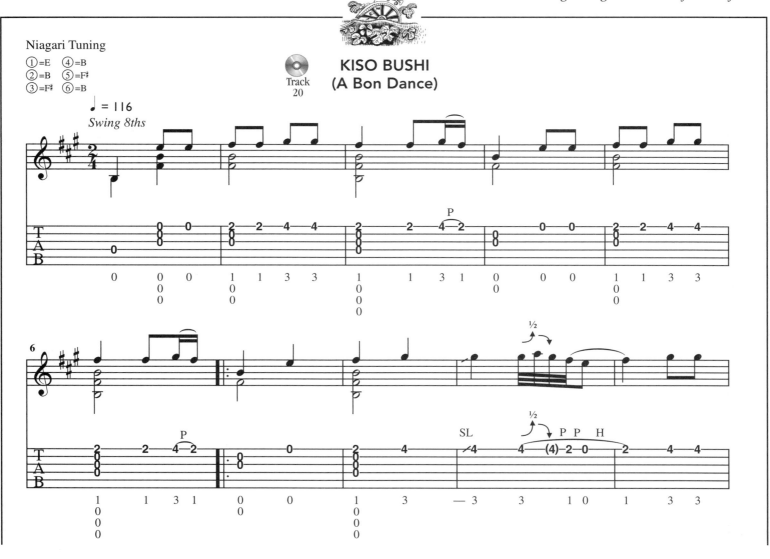

22

# Chapter 5   CLASSICAL MUSIC OF OKINAWA

Okinawa is the largest of the Ryukyu Islands, which lie between Taiwan and the Japanese island of Kyushu. The Ryukyu Kingdom was autonomous until 1609, when it fell under Japanese control. The kingdom continued to exist—developing a rich historical and cultural heritage of its own—until the Meiji Restoration, when Okinawa was formally annexed to Japan. The Ryukyu Islands constitute what is now known as the Okinawa Prefecture.

The classical music of Okinawa was inspired by the introduction of the Chinese san-hsien, or sanshin, as it would come to be known in Okinawa. In fact, Okinawa's classical music is known as *uta sanshin* ("songs of the sanshin"). In the time of the Ryukyu Kingdom, uta sanshin was performed for visiting envoys from China and for the Japanese courts. Although Okinawa's classical music features the sanshin, also used are the koto, taiko, and *kokyo* (which is like a sanshin that is bowed instead of plucked). A considerable amount of Okinawa's classical music has been compiled into a collection known as *Kun Kun Shi,* which consists of over 200 songs. Some of these songs were used in Ryukyu dance; "Shukkee Bushi" is one of these songs.

## "SHUKKEE BUSHI"

*Shukkee Bushi* means "the coming of dawn." This piece is considered a masterpiece of the *niagi* genre. *Niagi* (known as *niagari* in mainland Japan) refers to the tuning, which means "2nd tone raised," but it is also a type of lyrical song, full of emotion and longing. In the following arrangement, use a capo at the 5th fret for the best tone. The form of this tune alternates between verse and refrain. Also, watch out for the meter changes; the time signature alternates between $\frac{2}{4}$ and $\frac{3}{4}$ throughout the piece.

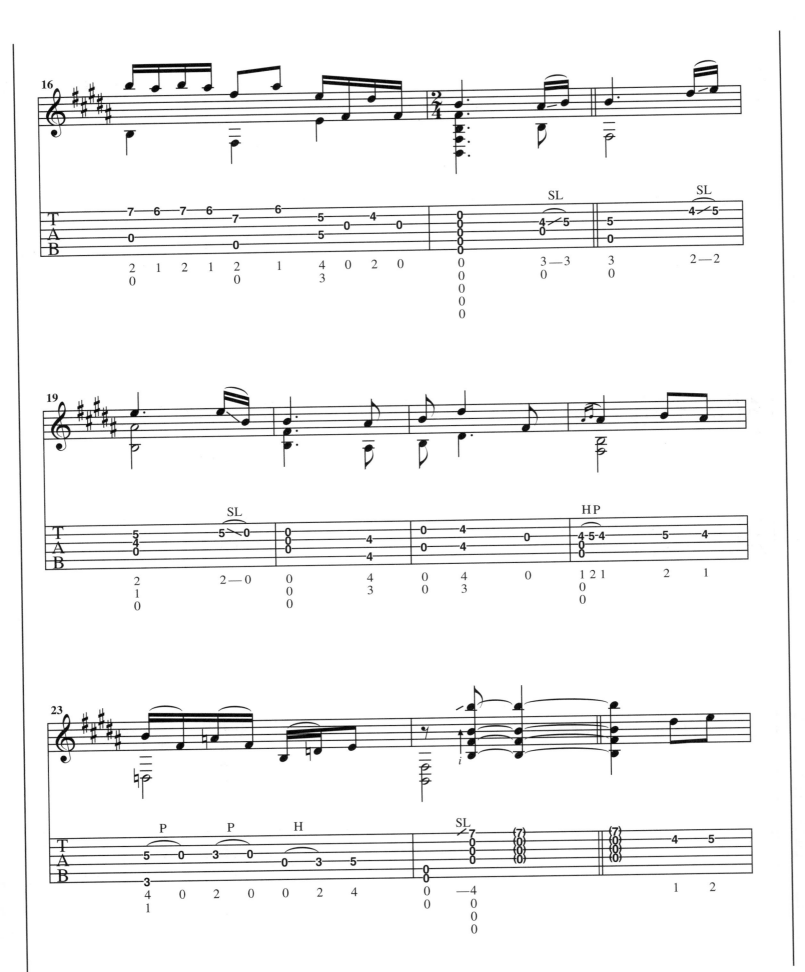

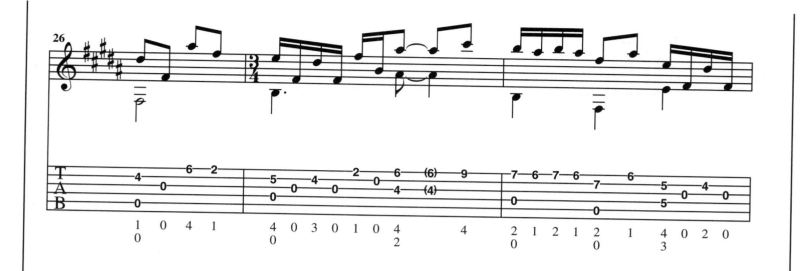

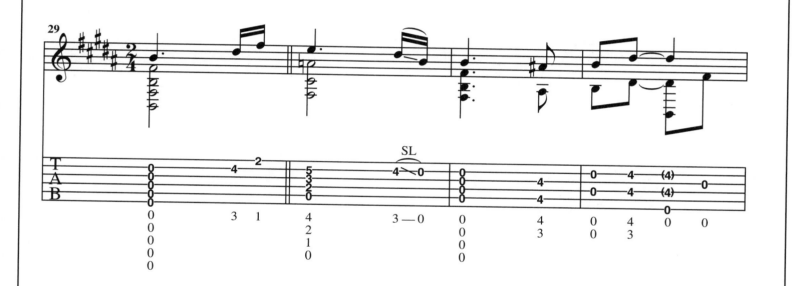

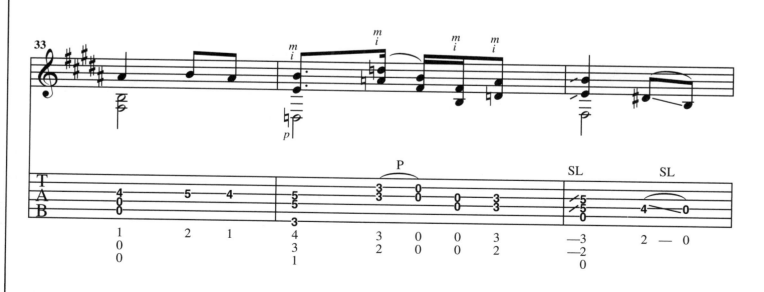

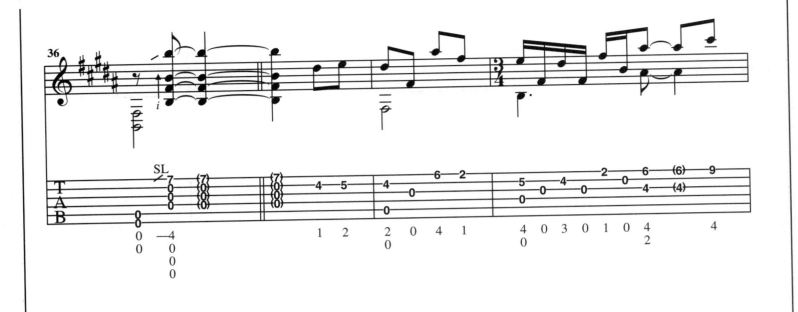

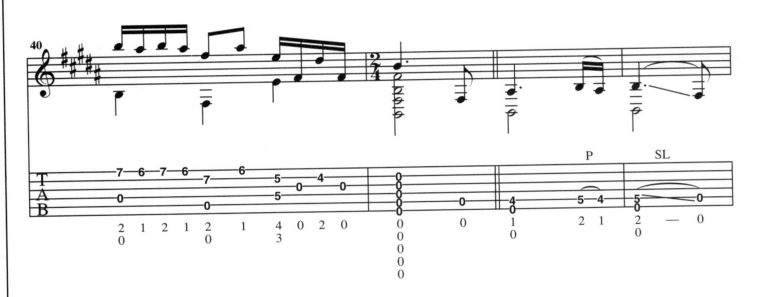

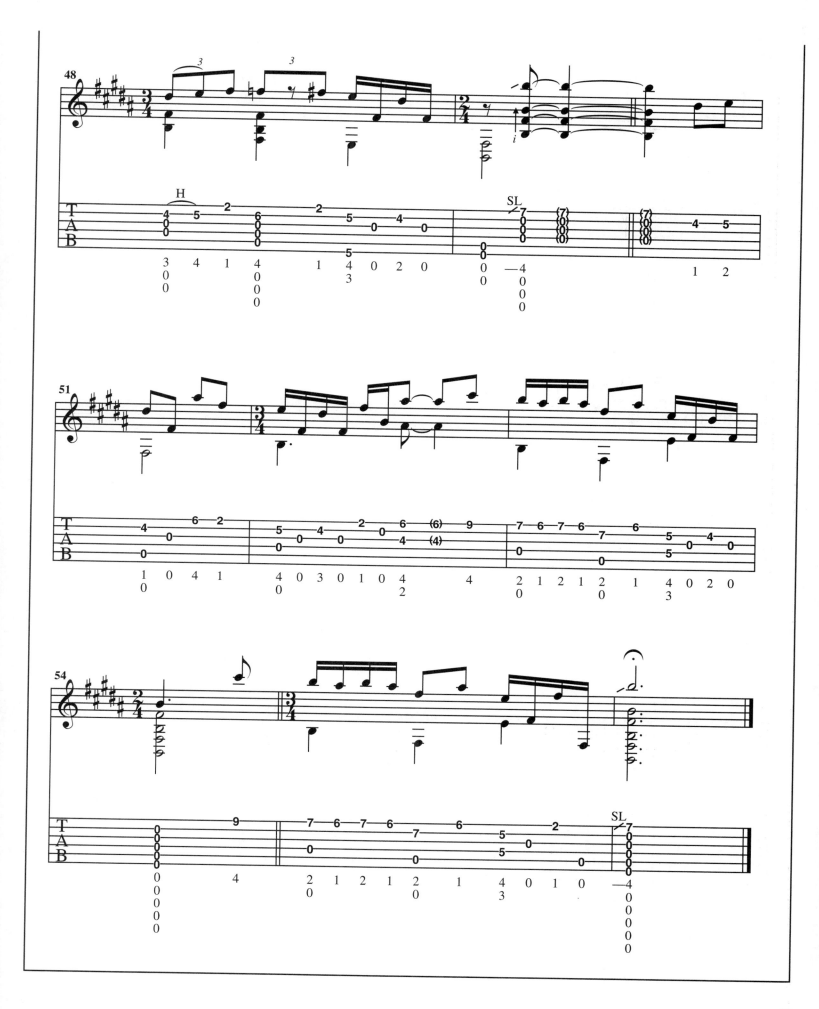

# Chapter 6 — SHAMISEN MUSIC OF THE KABUKI THEATER

JAPAN

There have been many different types of shamisen music used throughout the history of Kabuki. We will be looking at *naga-uta,* which means "long song." Specifically, we will look at a style of naga-uta known as *ozatsuma.* But first, let's take a brief look at Kabuki itself.

## WHAT IS KABUKI?

*Kabuki* is the traditional theater of Japan. It is a highly stylized form of drama performed through acting, dance, and singing. The actors wear *kumadori* makeup to exaggerate their expressions or to create animalistic or supernatural appearances (see page 39 for a painting of an actor in kumadori makeup). Although Kabuki was founded by a woman (see below), only male actors were allowed to perform for centuries. From early times, these dramas were filled with elaborate stage tricks such as revolving stages and trap doors for quick appearances and disappearances of actors. In some dramas, the actors would even be attached to wires and fly through the air. The stories themselves are filled with villains, clowns, samurai, and tragic lovers.

## IZUMO NO OKUNI

Izumo no Okuni (ca. 1572–1613) is recognized as the founder of Kabuki theater. She was a *miko* ("shrine maiden") at the Shinto Grand Shrine in Izumo. *Shinto,* which predates Buddhism in Japan, is an animistic religion centered around ancient Japanese gods (known as *kami*) and elemental spirits. Miko perform dances and assist the Shinto priests with various services at the shrine. In fiction, miko are often endowed with magical powers.

It was customary for miko, as well as Shinto priests, to travel abroad in search of donations for their shrine. Okuni traveled to Kyoto where she became known for a new kind of dance called *nembutsu,* which she would perform in the dry river beds. The suggestive dance would draw large crowds and became infamous for its sensuality.

In 1603, in a dry river bed of what is now known as the Kamo River, she gathered the social misfits, eccentrics, and outcasts known as *kabukimono* and taught them to dance, sing, and act. The term *kabukimono* is derived from *kabuku,* which means "to lean," or to be "out of the ordinary." So, Kabuki can be thought of as "experimental theater." In Okuni's troupe, women performed the parts of both men and women. Okuni herself was known for her portrayals of samurai and Christian priests. Okuni was eventually summoned to return to the shrine. However, though she always continued to send money, she never went back.

Okuni's Kabuki troupe eventually performed for the Imperial Court. Success at court spawned other troupes. Eventually, the shogunate—believing that the sensuality of the performances was a threat to public stability—banned women from the stage. Only older men were permitted to act on the Kabuki stage until after World War II, when women began to appear in roles, and even an all-woman troupe was formed. Kabuki fell out of favor for a while, along with other indigenous and important aspects of Japanese culture, in favor of European trends. However, as time went on, a renewed interest in traditional Japanese culture sparked a new appreciation for Kabuki, and it remains popular to this day.

# KABUKI MUSIC

The music of the Kabuki theater is highly structured, with minimal improvisation. It is performed by the shamisen and an ensemble known as *hayashi* (see also page 16). This ensemble consists of tsuzumi, taiko, *transverse* (side-blown) bamboo flutes known as *geza* and *nohkan*, and two types of wooden clappers known as *ki* and *tsuke*. The majority of Kabuki music is performed with vocals, but there are instrumental interludes performed by the shamisen that display great virtuosity and technique. These usually occur at dramatic peaks. They are often constructed from the 48 *ozatsuma patterns*, which are an important part of naga-uta Kabuki music. The patterns are used to create melodies and compositions, which the players memorize for each play.

There are nine sets of ozatsuma patterns:

1. **Jo**—Seven patterns used as preparatory or opening music

2. **Kakari**—Five patterns used for the beginnings of phrases

3. **Ji**—Twelve patterns used as accompaniment for recitations

4. **Te**—Six patterns used for introductions or endings (usually in free rhythm)

5. **Sanju**—Four patterns used for introductions and interludes; improvisation of these themes is allowed

6. **Tataki**—Two patterns used for cadences

7. **Otoshi**—Six brief patterns used for cadences

8. **Musubi**—Four patterns that progress towards cadences

9. **Dangire**—Two patterns used for cadences and final endings

The arrangement starting on page 32 is similar to an interlude you would hear in a Kabuki performance. It is composed using the ozatsuma patterns above. The patterns are labeled in the music so you can see how they would work together to make up a single composition. The piece is performed in its entirety on the CD, without a break. However, for easier listening access, each pattern is given its own track marker. The timing is very loose, or *rubato*, speeding up and slowing down when appropriate; the tempos given are meant only to be general indications. Watch for measures 47–52 and 59–64, where the *i* finger sounds the chords with alternating upstrokes and downstrokes. Also, be sure to tune your guitar to honchoshi tuning (see page 47) and place your capo at the 5th fret.

Remember, Kabuki is all about drama, and so is Kabuki music; be sure to listen to the CD for the full effect of this piece.

## OZATSUMA
### (Kabuki Interlude)

Honchoshi Tuning

①=E ④=B
②=B ⑤=E
③=E ⑥=B

Capo V

**Riyaku Sanju (Sanju 4)**

♩ = 88

*Rubato*

**Dangire Sanju (Sanju 3)**

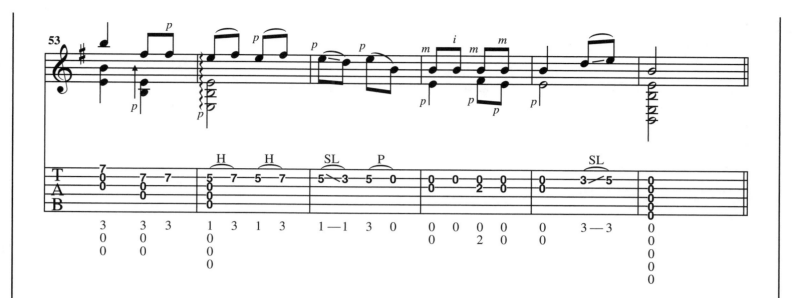

**Kinhiagejo (Jo 7)**

Track 28

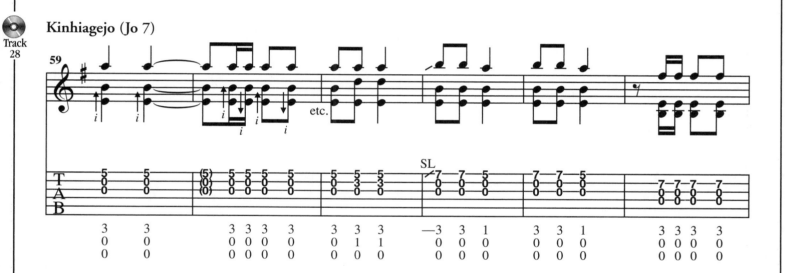

etc.

*rit.*

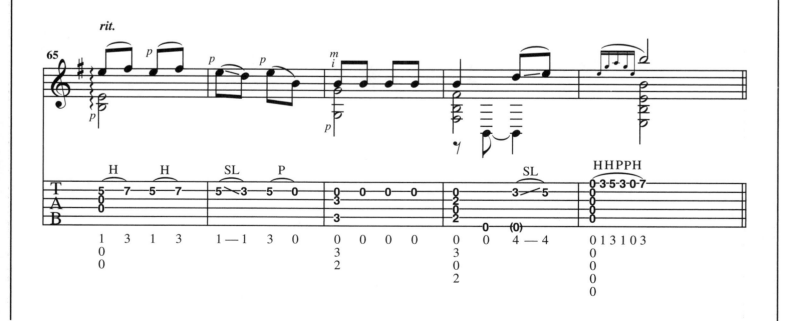

### Ryo Musubi Nagashi
### (Musubi 1)

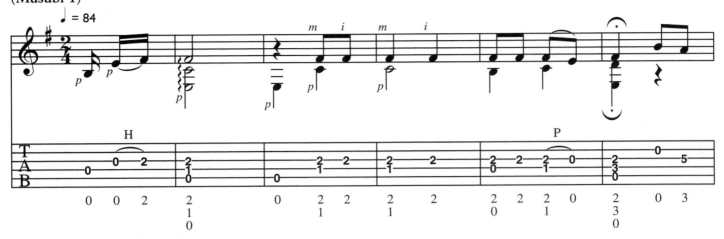

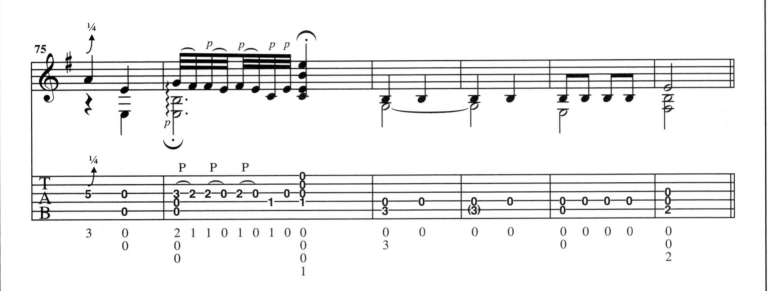

### Ritsu Musubi Nagashi
### (Musubi 2)

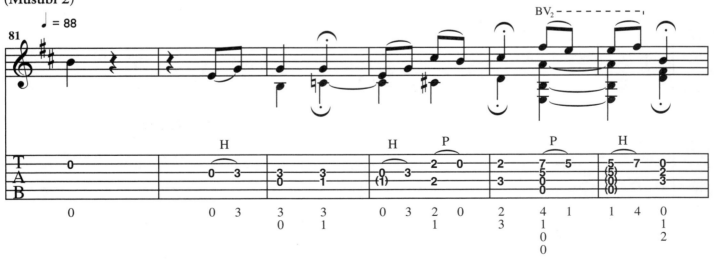

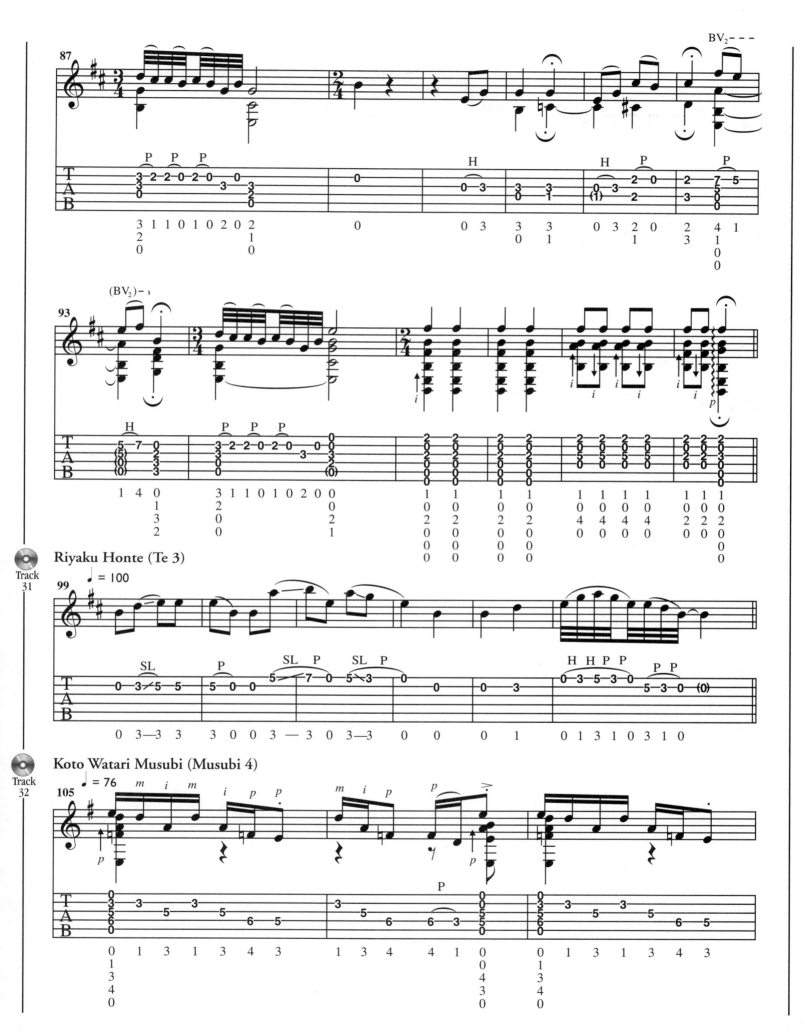

Riyaku Honte (Te 3)

Koto Watari Musubi (Musubi 4)

### Honte Oshigasanu (Te 2)

*molto accelerando*

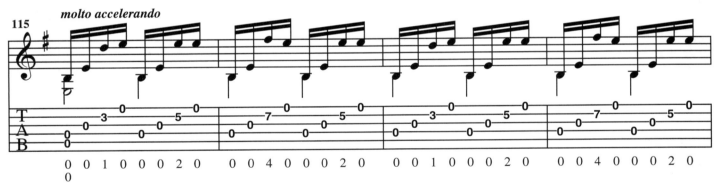

## Riyaku Dangire (Dangire 2)

Track 34

*Painting by Utagawa Kuniyoshi (1797–1861). Kabuki actors in full costume. The hero (bottom left) is wearing kumadori makeup; bright red stripes over a white base is standard for the hero's role.*

# Chapter 7 KOTO MUSIC (SOKYOKU)

**JAPAN**

## YATSUHASHI KENGYO AND THE MASTERS

Koto music, or *sokyoku,* began with Yatsuhashi Kengyo (1614–1685). Yatsuhashi was a blind musician who studied the shamisen before becoming a koto master. He was instrumental in making koto playing a profession of the blind. ("Kengyo" was an honorary title given to blind masters of the koto and shamisen.) Before him, it was not acceptable for men who were blind—or for *any* women—to play the koto. His efforts helped make koto playing available to the masses; he is known as the "father of sokyoku."

In the Later Ancient period, koto was played only in court as part of the gagaku ensemble. But, in the Heian period, there was a form of koto music known as *tsukushigoto,* which consisted of songs accompanied by the koto. In this style, the koto used tunings based on gagaku's ryo mode. Yatsuhashi Kengyo learned this form and then came up with his own. His new style was called *kumi-uta,* and like tsukushigoto, it consisted of "suites" of six short songs.

For this new style of music, Yatsuhashi devised new tunings and modes. The tunings were hirajoshi and kumoijoshi (see page 7)—both based on the *In* mode. These have remained the primary tunings and modes to this day. The majority of his pieces were in the kumi-uta style, though he also devised a style of instrumental, or *shirabe,* music. Most of these pieces were in the *danmono* style. (For an explanation of the danmono style, see "Rokudan no Shirabe," page 41).

There were other schools of sokyoku that followed Yatsuhashi, like that of Ikuta Kengyo and Yamada Kengyo, both of whom incorporated shamisen music into their compositions. At the end of the Edo period, Yoshizawa Kengyo created another form based on kumi-uta. The words to his songs were taken from ancient *waka,* or poems, from anthologies such as *Kokin Waka Shu.* He also devised a new tuning called kokinjoshi (page 7), which is based on a form of the *In* mode (and is thought by some to be based on both the *In* and *Yo* modes).

## MICHIO MIYAGI

With the Meiji Restoration came the introduction of Western music and ideas. A composer who had the most influence during this time was Michio Miyagi (1894–1956). His compositions featured new forms, techniques, and Western musical ideas. He also invented the *jushichigen,* a 17-string bass koto.

# INTRODUCTION TO "ROKUDAN NO SHIRABE" AND "MIDARE"

"Rokudan no Shirabe" and "Midare" are two of the oldest and most popular pieces of solo koto music. Both pieces were composed by Yatsuhashi Kengyo in the 17th century, and both fall into the shirabe, or instrumental, category. Let's take a closer look at each piece before playing the arrangements on the following pages.

## Rokudan no Shirabe

"Rokudan no Shirabe" is the oldest known piece of solo koto music. The title translates roughly to "Music in Six Steps." It belongs to the *danmono* tradition, which divides the composition into equal sections. *Dan* means "section," and *roku* means "six." In the danmono style, each section consists of 104 beats (26 measures). This is the case with "Rokudan no Shirabe," except for the first dan, which has an extra four beats. The danmono style is a kind of *theme and variations,* with the first section serving as the theme and the sections that follow as the variations. When performed, each section starts slow. The tempo increases and peaks in the middle of the dan, then slows back down so that the end of the section is as slow as the beginning.

"Rokudan no Shirabe" ("Rokudan" for short) can be performed in many ways. It can be a solo koto piece (which is how it is most well known). It is also a popular piece to play on the shamisen. It can be performed as a duet with koto and shakuhachi, koto and shamisen, or shamisen and shakuhachi. It can also be performed as a trio with koto, shamisen, and shakuhachi.

All the fundamental techniques of koto playing are used in "Rokudan," which makes it a great practice piece for students. Hirajoshi tuning is used throughout the composition.

On page 42 is the first dan of "Rokudan." The cross-string technique (see page 18) is featured prominently in this arrangement. Pay close attention to the left-hand fingering and ties, making sure that all notes ring out for their full value. A capo at the 4th fret brings the guitar closer to the koto's tonal range.

## Midare

"Midare" is also considered to be in the danmono style. However, this is the only danmono piece that has sections of unequal length, without the standard amount of beats. It is also supposed to be performed in a free and unconstrained way, hence the title of the piece, "Midare," which means "disorder" or "unorthodox." This piece shows how adventurous and innovative Yatsuhashi was; though he lived in a strict feudal society, he was never afraid to break the rules.

Like "Rokudan," "Midare" can be performed as a solo koto piece or as duets and trios of various combinations. Certain parts of "Midare" are believed to represent heavy snow falling in the forest.

On page 44 is the first dan of "Midare." There are bends in measures 21, 23, and 24. This is to emulate the sound of the koto string being pushed down, thereby causing a fluctuation of pitch. These measures also feature different runs, which may sound odd to Western ears but are standard to the koto sound. Again, the cross-string technique is featured prominently in this arrangement.

# ROKUDAN NO SHIRABE
## (Music in Six Steps)

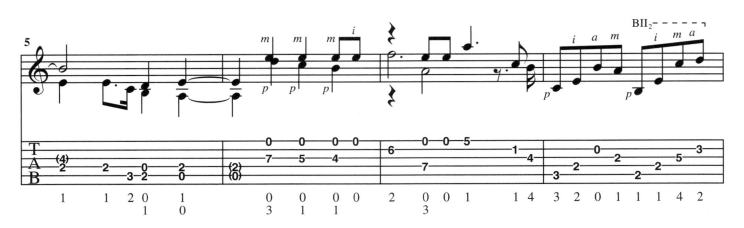

*accelerando poco a poco*

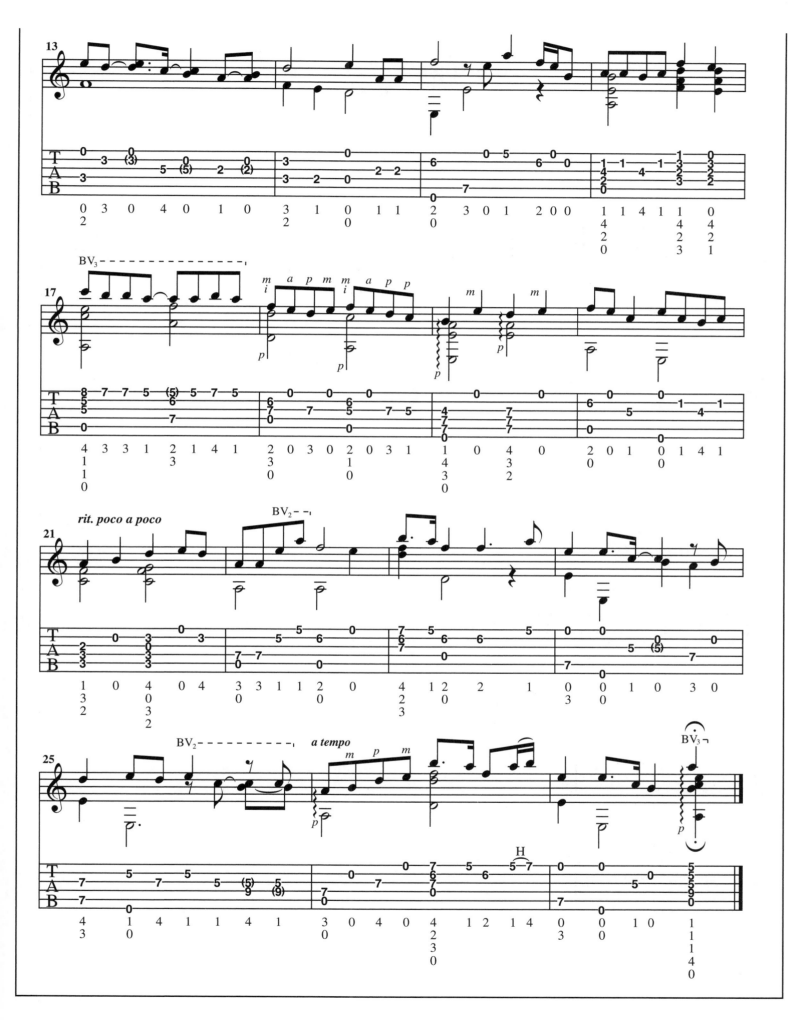

## MIDARE
### (Disorder)

Track 36

# Final Word

Thank you for taking the time to read and play through this book; it was a pleasure for me to write. As I mentioned previously, traditional Japanese music is so rich historically, sociologically, and artistically, that it could take a lifetime to study. I hope this introduction opens the door for you to further explore this wonderful and complex musical heritage. Following is a list of books and recordings so you can continue your journey. If you have any comments or questions, write to: burgess_speed@hotmail.com.

*Enjoy.*

## REFERENCES FOR FURTHER READING

Ackermann, Peter. *Kumiuta: Traditional Songs for Certificates (A Study of Their Texts and Implications).* Bern: Peter Lang Publishers, Inc., 1990.

Hisao, Tanabe. *Japanese Music.* Tokyo: Kokusai Bunka Shinkokai, 1959.

Markham, Elizabeth J. *Saibara: Japanese Court Songs of the Heian Period* (two volumes). Cambridge University Press, 1983.

Shigeo, Kishibe. *The Traditional Music of Japan.* Tokyo: Kokusai Bunka Shinkokai (The Society for International Cultural Relations), 1966.

### On the Web

http://en.wikipedia.org/wiki/music_of_japan
http://en.wikipedia.org/wiki/Kabuki
http://web-japan.org/nipponia/nipponia22/en/topic/index.html
http://www.mamalisa.com/world/japan.html
http://www.wonder-okinawa.jp/014/en/1c-m/index9.html
http://www.komuso.com/index.html
http://asnic.utexas.edu/asnic/countries/japan/japmusic.html
http://www.creative-arts.net/kabuki/Breakdown/Patterns.htm
http://www.wsu.edu/~dee/ancjapan/music.htm

To see a performance of "Sakura":
http://www.youtube.com/watch?v=syOL9ZhQO98

To see a performance of "Midare":
http://www.youtube.com/watch?v=dhxlQlZafvY

## REFERENCES FOR FURTHER LISTENING

*Folk Music of Japan.* New York: Ethnic Folkways Library, Smithsonian Folkways Records (P429), 1952.

*Japan: Traditional Vocal And Instrumental Music (Shakuhachi, Biwa, Koto, Shamisen).* Soloists of the Ensemble Nipponia, Nonesuch, 1990 (original release, 1976).

*Japanese Masterpieces for the Shakuhachi.* New York: Lyrichord (LYRCD 7176).

*Japanese Work Songs.* "Music of Japanese People" (series), World Music Library, 1994.

*Music of Okinawa.* "Music of Japanese People" (series), World Music Library, 1994.

*The Traditional Music of Japan.* Yokohama: Victor, 1965.

*The Very Best of Japanese Music: Shakuhachi, Koto, Taiko Drums...* New York: Arc Music (EUCD1861), 2004.

# Appendix

## ALTERNATE GUITAR TUNINGS USED IN THIS BOOK

Following are the two *alternate tunings* used in this book. An alternate tuning is any tuning *other* than *standard tuning* (E–A–D–G–B–E). These are derived from the shamisen tunings on page 6. The CD includes tuning tracks for both tunings, so you can be sure the pitches are correct.

### Honchoshi

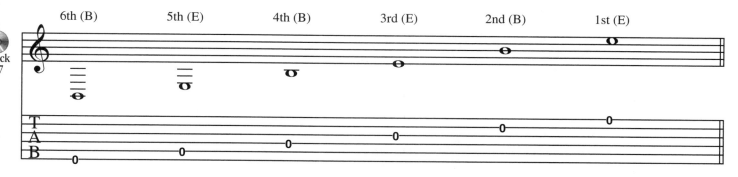

Track 37

6th (B)    5th (E)    4th (B)    3rd (E)    2nd (B)    1st (E)

### Niagari

Track 38

6th (B)    5th (F♯)    4th (B)    3rd (F♯)    2nd (B)    1st (E)